AF439619

HOW TO GAIN TRUST

HOW TO GAIN TRUST BACK IN A RELATIONSHIP

All rights reserved. No part of this publication may be reproduced, distributed, or transmitted in any form or by any means, including photocopying, recording, or other electronic or mechanical methods, without the prior written permission of the publisher, except in the case of brief quotations embodied in critical reviews and certain other noncommercial uses permitted by copyright law.

Copyright © Philips Felix, 2022.

Table of content

Chapter 1

As the old saying goes, trust is the cornerstone of any relationship, yet that trust may, sadly, be damaged. Often it's due to adultery, and other times it's a consequence of one spouse doing something that breaches the other partner's feeling of safety and trust. Trust may also be lost when any form of expectation in a relationship isn't honored, says Antoinette Beauchamp, certified professional life coach. This frequently becomes the case since these expectations sadly are not always conveyed with the other person, and as a consequence, boundaries get crossed. Whatever the root of this reduced feeling of confidence in the relationship may be, hope is not lost. You can repair trust in a relationship, but doing so does need effort from all individuals involved.

But, before we get ahead of ourselves, it's necessary to first comprehend what trust genuinely is, and what it looks and feels like in the scope of a relationship. Beauchamp sees it as a sensation of dedication and faith—kind of like a gigantic, loving embrace. "Trust feels comfortable, pleasurable, and secure," she continues. "You feel that you can consistently rely and depend on your partner in times of need. No matter what is up in the air, you have a firm foundation and somewhere to land."

So with that in mind, take stock of whether you think you have a healthy base of trust in your relationship. And if not? Keep reading for warning signals and professional ideas for how to restore the trust that's been lost.

Signs of lack of trust in a relationship
A loss of trust will look and feel different for every couple and in every relationship, but here are numerous symptoms warning that the trust may have gone MIA.

You frantically cling to your lover and never want to let them out of sight.
You don't allow yourself to be vulnerable or to become close to someone out of fear of being injured.
You feel a great weight of doubt and unease.
You doubt the person's conduct and feel like they're concealing something. You may even feel driven to spy through their messages or DMs.

Rebuilding trust in a relationship

1. Have a willingness to work on the relationship

Just like it takes two to dance, you can't repair trust by yourself. "This signals that the one who betrayed the trust is eager to demonstrate how they want to engage in the relationship and fix the brokenness," says Lauren Cook, a marriage and family therapist. "The one whose trust was violated is also willing to forgive and make oneself vulnerable once again for a repaired connection." So, the first step in rebuilding trust is to simply check in and make sure both parties are on board and are willing to put in the work to make it happen.

2. Openly apologize

In addition to having the desire, building trust demands a sincere apology. "While it can be normal for the person who breached their partner's trust to feel protective, this just aggravates the pain in the relationship," Cook continues. "Whether it's a letter, a meaningful conversation, several discussions, or another means to send an apology, it's vital that the person exhibits remorse and a commitment to restore the relationship."

3. Reflect on the experience

To reestablish confidence in the partnership, both sides must also take some time to introspect, assess their emotional space, and extract a lesson from the occurrence. "Spend time concentrating on what it is that caused you or your partner pain," Beauchamp says. "Reflect on the activities committed that shattered the confidence, to begin with. What did it make you feel? How are you feeling now as a consequence of all that happened?"

4. Create new memories

The next step is to focus on developing new enjoyable experiences together. "A fantastic experience will shift the attitude for any couple," Beauchamp says. "Do something that can make you laugh, smile, and connect nicely," Cook thinks that these fresh memories will promote optimism in the relationship and remind both sides that they are capable of having pleasant interactions.

5. Remember that people may be trusted

When someone betrays your trust, it's normal to distrust all of your ties, romantic and otherwise. But, be cautious to not allow oneself to get locked in this negative loop. "Look at your other relationships with family, friends, and other connections, and remind yourself that the majority of people want to be kind and want to keep your trust," Cook recommends.

6. Ask for what you need

Communication is vital when you're working on establishing your relationship. That's why Beauchamp suggests getting honest with yourself about what you need your partner to do to regain trust. What may help you feel more supported and comfortable in the relationship? Once you realize this, discuss those requests honestly and freely with your partner.

7. Be willing to be exposed
There surely is strength in vulnerability—especially in relationships. "Put your walls down and your ego aside," Beauchamp urges. "Vulnerability creates vulnerability and enhances connection. Creating unique experiences may aid in assistance and mend what's broken."

8. Reignite the relationship
Instead of interpreting lost trust as a relationship speed bump, consider it as an opportunity for a fresh start. Beauchamp suggests using this time to rekindle the flame between you and your sweetheart. One technique to attain this is to discover each other's love language (there's a free quiz for that) and actively supply one other with what is needed to feel cherished, protected, and supported in the partnership.

9. Focus on the future

To leave the past behind you, both you and your partner must concentrate on what's ahead rather than obsessing on prior blunders. Beauchamp's advice is to have an open and honest discourse about how you both want to move forward into a new chapter in your partnership. Design a vision of your future together and how you want it to be, and touch on both the short-term and long-term objectives.

How Can Trust Be Broken In a Relationship?

Most persons consider trust as the key component of a good relationship. It's necessary to be vulnerable, create connections, and keep a sense of safety. Healthy relationships are predicated on integrity or doing what you say you will do. When this is not maintained, the safety, confidence, and support of a steady relationship are destroyed, at least briefly.

Trust in a relationship may be eroded by the following:

Not following through on a promise
Not accepting responsibility for heinous deeds
Withholding love and/or affection
Lack of physical or emotional connectedness
Addictive habits (i.e., drugs, alcohol, pornography, gambling) (i.e., drugs, alcohol, pornography, gambling) (i.e., drugs, alcohol, pornography, gambling)
Infidelity (both asexual and nonsexual affair) (both asexual and nonsexual affairs) (both asexual and nonsexual affairs)
Being directly scolded or your partner speaking poorly about you behind your back
Hitting an emotional "raw spot"

How to Know When Rebuilding Is Possible
There are various indications to look for that tell you whether it may be achievable to repair confidence once it's been lost. For example, both parties must be willing to work on the relationship and the major purpose should be to reestablish a sense of safety.

Rebuilding trust in a relationship is doable, but only if:

The wounded person is given time to make an informed decision on how to recover trust and develop the relationship
They make a conscious decision to forgive
They're able to acquire the emotional muscle to not engage in a destructive phase of inquiry and defensiveness
Simple queries about the betrayal are answered so a larger detrimental image isn't produced and they want to know more is lessened
Both parties strive to work on the relationship.
The basic purpose is to restore safety in the partnership.

One partner shares all unavoidable contacts with an affair partner

20 Ways to Rebuild Trust In a Relationship

The good news is that even after a devastating betrayal like adultery, a trust may be rebuilt. Not only that, betrayal is sometimes the catalyst for rejuvenating a relationship that was in significant trouble even before the betrayal occurred. Healing is a process, but when two people are engaged in learning, making apologies, and recommitting, magic may happen.

Chapter 2

Here are twenty techniques to reestablish trust in a relationship:

1. Make a Commitment

Both spouses need to commit 100 percent to perform the work necessary in mending following a betrayal. It is a long-term investment, depending on the sort of betrayal, but knowing the relationship is worth fighting for is the commitment both couples need to make.

2. Both Partners Take Responsibility

Commitment from the betrayer involves showing to your spouse that you are sincerely remorseful and prepared to work on winning back trust, no matter what it takes. Commitment from the betrayed entails attentive listening to the betrayer as well as analyzing any of their actions that may have led to suffering in the relationship previous to the betrayal.

3. Refine Your Communication Style

Asking your spouse open-ended questions is a terrific technique to improve emotional intimacy and reestablish trust. It stimulates deep discourse as these questions can't be addressed with a simple "Yes" or "No." How you choose to convey issues is what counts. Learning how to self-soothe may help both the speaker and the listener to survive the tension to digest the betrayal.

4. Accept Repair Attempts

Rebuilding trust primarily boils down to select if you desire retribution or a relationship. After a real apology is delivered, worldwide marriage expert, Dr. John Gottman, believes that when betrayed spouses don't accept these repair efforts, there is an increased probability of divorce.

5. Set a Time to Talk About the Betrayal
It's crucial to create a daily period (15-20 minutes) to speak about the betrayal; else, it may be a 24/7 debate. This helps each person to prepare for a fruitful talk as well as acquire control of any emotions that may surface unexpectedly. Evaluate progress regularly to determine when to lessen the frequency of the sessions.

6. Set Time for a Non-Negotiable Weekly Marriage Meeting

A weekly marriage meeting is an excellent practice to improve a couple. This is a committed time, to be honest, and discuss major difficulties in the relationship. Good subjects to talk about include thankfulness, things that did/did not go well over the week (in a non-critical and non-defensive style), housework, money, external responsibilities, date evenings, etc.

7. Redefine New Marriage Rules

Having self-imposed restrictions might allow the betrayed spouse to have a feeling of control while regaining trust. Self-imposed norms are liberated as they are non-negotiable and formed jointly. These might entail establishing limits and regular check-ins to minimize issues from worsening.

8. Create a Culture of Appreciation
Couples who discover methods to show gratitude for one another frequently have a stronger chance of restoring shattered trust. This is about sharing a "we-ness" or togetherness vs. separateness.

9. Glorify the Struggle
Glorifying the battle implies showing pride that you've weathered huge obstacles in your relationship. Actively talking about your commitment to one another vs. doubting if you made the proper decision is crucial in repairing trust.

10. Stop All Contact With the Affair Partner
If there is ongoing communication with the affair partner, rehabilitation will be severely delayed. This involves ending all physical, emotional, and verbal closeness. If the affair partner is a co-worker, the relationship must be completely business.

11. Share Any Necessary or Unplanned Encounters With the Affair Partner
This implies there is an atmosphere of complete transparency if inevitable contact with the affair partner needs to be made. This comes along with a desire to honestly answer any queries your spouse may have.

12. Don't Gossip About or Trash Talk Your Partner to Others
Gossiping and trash-talking create an added layer of stress, especially when the goal is to work on your relationship. It can be tempting to vent or want to vent, but it boils down to knowing that what you focus on expands, so choose who you talk to and how you talk about your partner wisely.

13. Tell the True Story of the Betrayal

Telling the story of the affair isn't easy for either partner, but it will allow you and your partner to understand what happened and why. The damaged spouse mustn't participate in a harmful process of inquiry and defensiveness, which never helps to heal, even if the answers are accurate. Instead, begin by addressing the plain facts.

14. Create an Environment of Proactive Transparency

Our emotions might come in the way of speaking the truth and hearing the truth. Transparency puts everything out in the open to foster trust and minimize overthinking in the connection. Proactive transparency means making the extra effort to emphasize crucial elements about the betrayal without waiting to be investigated or asked. This creates trust and indicates a willingness to be held responsible.

15. Understand the Power of Vulnerability

In being vulnerable, you may build a sense of emotional safety with your spouse. It's the fundamental technique to build a marital tie and keep love alive. It's how you'll be able to re-establish a stable emotional relationship and retain intimacy in your marriage. This goes hand-in-hand with proactive openness.

16. Evaluate Your Questions

To raise productive inquiries, the betrayed spouse has to stop and ponder. According to infidelity expert, Dr. Talal H. Alsaleem, PsyD, LMFT, appropriate inquiries require thinking about how your query will assist to understand what occurred and why it happened. The idea is to ask intelligent questions that inspire helpful replies.

17. Evaluate Your Answers

The betrayer needs to answer any questions truthfully, but also with the lowest level of detail possible. The idea is to prevent any terrible pictures the deceived may have to cope with later on. Cheating has been related to symptoms akin to post-traumatic stress disorder (PTSD), therefore too many graphic details may place a strain on the recovery process.

18. Take Time to Forgive

It takes time to properly comprehend why a betrayal took place, thus cutting the healing process short will not allow for good rehabilitation to take place. In other words, avoidance is never a strategy for healing, nor is forgiving too quickly. Building a solid connection with your spouse entails spending as much time as possible to thoroughly process and work on improved coping techniques to restore the relationship.

19. Seek Professional Help

Often, a couple is so overwhelmed that they don't know where to begin. This is where couples counseling may be crucial. They can help both the betrayed and the betrayer to ask and answer questions in a manner that supports rehabilitation. They may provide couples with structure and a plan of action to slow down the process of healing to a productive pace.

20. Plan, Plan, Plan

Work together to build a strategy to avoid such breaches of trust. Be open to finding areas that may have fostered distrust (withholding financial information, not sharing information in your everyday life, spending too much time outside of the relationship, etc) (withholding financial information, not sharing information in your daily living, spending too much time outside of the relationship, etc). Plan to enhance friendship, develop rituals of connection, and construct a new relationship together.

Chapter 3

Losing someone's trust may be devastating for everyone affected. While it's not always straightforward, getting someone to trust you again is feasible if you're patient and attentive. Whether it's a friend, family member, or lover, there are things you may do to get back your confidence.

1. Using Actions to Build Trust:\sAllow the other person to have space. When you break someone's confidence, it could cause both of you to feel offended. You might be feeling guilty, while the other person can be feeling sad or irritated. Remember that they may require some room to heal.

Naturally, you wish to address the situation fast. But respect the other person's desire for space.

You may try declaring, "Amy, I sincerely want to start working on our relationship. But I understand if you need to take some time."

Be respectful of limitations. If someone wants you not to call for a few days, then allow them to have the time out that they need.

Be dependable. Your comments are incredibly vital when striving to restore confidence. Your acts are equally crucial. You may prove that you are trustworthy by being dependable.

Do what you say you will do. If you resolve to cease being late all the time, show that you have changed by being punctual. Call when you say you will. Remember, you're aiming to rebuild trust. Make a point to stick to everything that you say you will do, even if it's merely making a phone call.

Show that you can be counted on. If your boss needs you to submit any critical papers, get the job done accurately, and on time.

Practice the three A's. If you are wanting to restore a love connection, you could take some further steps to show your partner how much you care. The three A's are Affection, Attention, and Appreciation. Figure out techniques to show these feelings daily.

There are numerous ways to be loving. For example, make it a point to deliver a hug when your partner comes home from work.

You may pay attention by being mindful of the small things. If you observe that your friend wants more coffee, bring it without being asked.

Use sentences to indicate how much you appreciate the other person. You may say something like, "I sincerely admire how sensitive you are."

Take up additional responsibilities. One technique to establish that you are trustworthy is by going the extra mile. Whether you are rebuilding trust in a personal or professional connection, adopting new obligations is a fantastic technique to restore trust. It shows you are willing to work hard.

Maybe you are seeking to convince your boss to trust you again. Volunteer to stay late if he needs someone to help with the end-of-month reports.

If you are striving to restore confidence in a friendship, consider going out of your way to do something kind. For example, deliver lunch to your pal when you know she's having a difficult day at work.

Perhaps you are working on your connection with your spouse. Try washing the dishes or taking out the trash without being asked.

Be yourself. When you are seeking to restore trust, it is vital to show that you are willing to make improvements. However, it is vital to show that you are serious. Don't seek to fully modify your personality.

Changing too much won't appear honest. For example, if you're striving to rebuild your parents' trust, don't abruptly begin acting like a different kid.

For example, maybe your parents want you to help out more around the house. That doesn't indicate you should stop hanging out with your mates altogether. It just signifies that you should endeavor to strike a balance.

Don't strive to adjust your personality. If you've always been able to joke with buddies, don't stop now. Becoming completely serious all of the time will not seem honest.

2 Apologizing Effectively

Gather your thoughts. It could be daunting to make a serious apology. It's alright to feel anxious. Take some time to plan and pick out what you want to say.

Make a list of your important points. This list should comprise an apology, an acceptance of responsibility, and a statement of how you plan to make amends.

Practice what you want to say. You may try the apology out loud while gazing in the mirror.

Ask for time to talk. Try mentioning, "Lauren, I know you're upset with me. Is there a time this week when we could sit down and have a conversation?"

Express your feelings. If you want to restore someone's trust, you have to have a meaningful talk with them. If you have wronged someone, the correct thing to do is apologize. Begin by stating how you feel.

If you are wanting to reestablish a friendship, tell your pal how you are feeling. You may say, "Sue, I feel truly bad that I shattered your confidence. I know it would be tough, but I would like for us to focus on restoring our connection."

State your intentions. If you are chatting with a love connection try stating, "I want us to be able to trust one another and I will do what it takes to make that happen."

Be honest. Whatever you say during your apology, make sure that you mean it. The other person may be able to identify if you're lying, and it would merely further destroy your relationship.

Accept responsibility. If you are apologizing, then you have something to be sorry for. To rebuild someone's trust, you need to demonstrate that you acknowledge what you did wrong. Your apology should incorporate an acknowledgment of your conduct.

Make it evident that you know what you did wrong. If you are looking to restore trust in a professional connection, you should present actual examples.

Be honest. If you're going to restore trust after this, the other person needs to know that you're being forthright and honest about everything that occurred.

Try expressing, "I made a mistake when I did not properly review the materials. I know it costs the company money." This demonstrates that you recognize the repercussions of your action.

You should also employ special circumstances when chatting to a pal. For example, you may say, "John, it was bad of me to lie and pretend I had to work late. If I'm going out with other mates, I should just be honest and tell you that."

Actively listen. A constructive conversation has more than one participant. After you have expressed what you want to say, give the other person a chance. Take efforts to convey that you are listening and empathize with them.

Use your body language. Nod your head and make eye contact while the other person is talking.

Rephrase the main elements. This will suggest that you are retaining what is being communicated.

For example, you may say, "I hear you stating that you have lost faith in me and that it will take time to restore that trust."

Actively listen. A constructive conversation has more than one participant. After you have expressed what you want to say, give the other person a chance. Take efforts to convey that you are listening and empathize with them.

Use your body language. Nod your head and make eye contact while the other person is talking.

Rephrase the main elements. This will suggest that you are retaining what is being communicated.

For example, you may say, "I hear you admitting that you have lost faith in me and that it will take time to restore that trust

Write a letter. A face-to-face apology is always the nicest option. Unfortunately, it is not always practicable. Maybe you live far away from the other person, or maybe they are not keen to chat with you. If such is the case, you could try an apology letter.

Write a handwritten letter. This is more personal than an e-mail. You should never make an important apology via SMS.

Edit your letter. It might take you a handful of iterations to get the perfect tone and content.

Your letter should be brief and to the point. Try to make it approximately 3 paragraphs. Your first paragraph should express the apology, the second should admit responsibility, and the third may detail how you would wish to fix the problem.

3. Moving Forward

Be patient. When you initially started this relationship, trust was not immediate. Trust has to be earned over time. It is common that when trust is damaged, it may take some time to repair.

Try not to rush the process. Acknowledge that the other person might take time to start trusting you again.

State your point. Try stating, "I recognize that this operation might take time. I understand. Take all of the time you need."

Try not to dwell on the scenario. It's vital, but once you have apologized and begun taking attempts to repair the trust, you don't need to worry over the situation consistently.

Acknowledge emotions. If you are seeking to reestablish a personal connection, it might feel like a very hard operation. You are likely going to feel a wide assortment of emotions. Remember that the other person might be emotional, too.

It is normal for you to feel guilt, grief, despair, and frustration. Permit oneself to feel a wide array of emotions.

Acknowledge your emotions and move on. Say to yourself, "Today I'm feeling rather guilty. But I know I'm taking efforts to remedy it, so I can't be too hard on myself."

Understand that your friend is probably experiencing a huge array of feelings. They might feel offended, enraged, or sad. That is normal.

Create a new connection. When confidence has been shattered, it is viable to repair the relationship. However, it is vital to realize that the dynamics might vary. Be prepared to have a different connection than before.
Maybe you have exploited your boss's confidence. Be prepared to accept a smaller degree of responsibility at work for a spell.

If you have breached the trust in your love relationship, you might not be as close as you were before. Your partner may not trust you with intimate thoughts for a while.
Perhaps you are coping with a damaged relationship. You may have to accept the fact that your friendship is more superficial than it was before.

Prepare for numerous outcomes. If you violate someone's trust, there is a significant possibility that you can make amends. But you should recognize that the relationship might be damaged beyond repair. Try to mentally prepare for a variety of eventualities.

Accept the possibility that you may have to move on. If someone doesn't want to be your friend anymore, you can't force them.

Try to uncover something positive in your life to focus on. Make a list of all of the things you have going for you.

Spend time with other people. Focus on enhancing the relationships that you still have.

www.ingramcontent.com/pod-product-compliance
Lightning Source LLC
Chambersburg PA
CBHW071500150726
48000CB00006B/2639